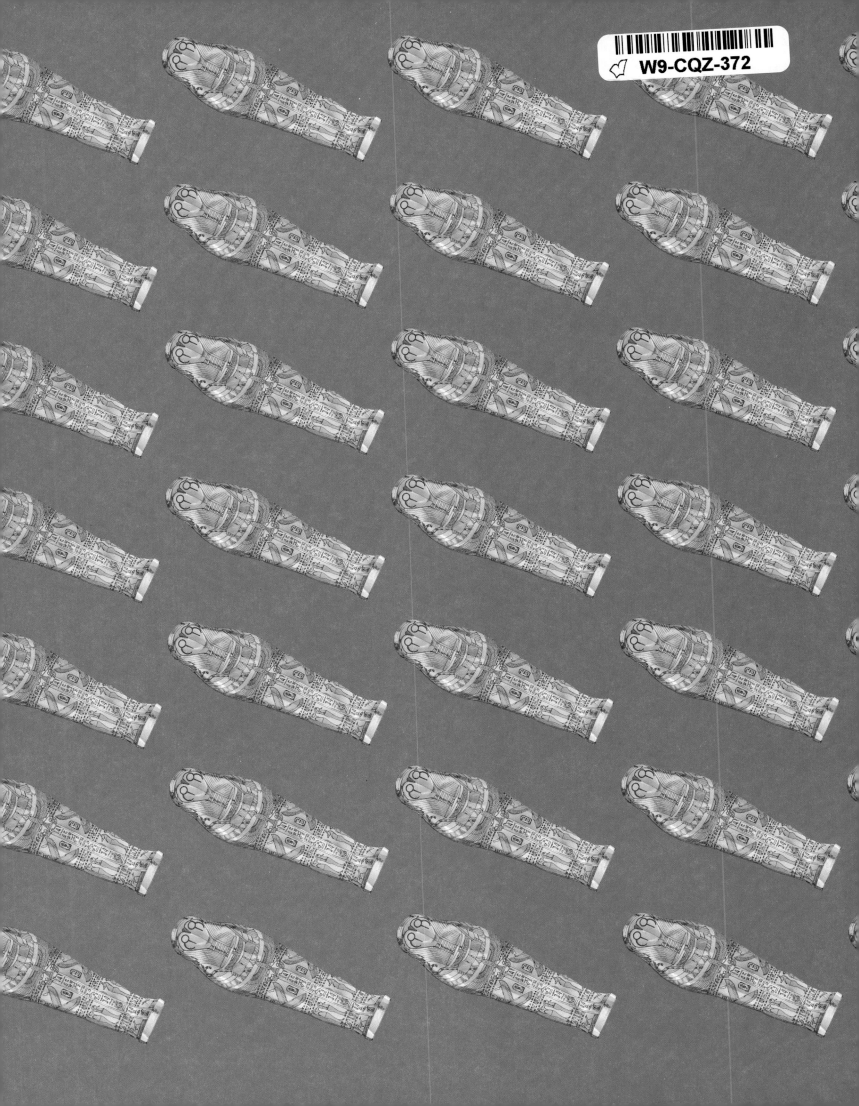

the world of the
PHARAOH

the world of the PHARAOH

Anne Millard

Illustrations by
L.R. Galante

PETER BEDRICK BOOKS
NEW YORK

Published by
PETER BEDRICK BOOKS
a division of NTC/Contemporary
Publishing Group, Inc.
4255 West Touhy Avenue,
Lincolnwood (Chicago),
Illinois, 60712-1975

Text and illustrations
© 1998 Macdonald Young Books,
an imprint of Wayland Publishers Limited

Commissioning editor: Dereen Taylor
Editor: Ruth Thomson
Designer: Edward Kinsey
Picture Researcher: Kate Davenport

Library of Congress Cataloguing-in-Publication Data
Millard, Anne.
  The world of the pharaoh / Anne Millard : illustrations by L.R.
Gallante. --1st ed.
     p.   cm.
  Summary: A cultural history of life in ancient Egypt, including
the rights and powers of the pharaohs, religion, agriculture, the
arts, mummification, the pyramids, temple ceremonies, magic,
and medicine.
  ISBN 0-87226-292-8 (hardcover)
  1. Egypt--Civilization--To 332 B.C.--Juvenile literature.
[1. Egypt--Civilization--To 332 B.C.] I. Gallante, L. R. , 111.
II. Title.
DT61.M5524 1998
932'.01--dc21   98-28851
                                          CIP
                                           AC

Printed and bound in Portugal
by Edições ASA

Second Printing, 1999

ANNE MILLARD

Anne Millard fell in love with ancient Egypt when she was only 4 years old and has been studying it ever since. She has degrees in History and Education as well as in Egyptology. She has worked for the Egypt Exploration Society, and participated in their excavations in Egypt. She lectures for the Extra-Mural Department of London University, besides writing numerous books on history and archaeology.

STUDIO GALANTE

Formed in 1995 and based in Florence, Italy, Studio Galante consists of four young illustrators L.R.Galante, Manuela Cappon, Francesco Spadoni and Allessandro Menchi. The studio is internationally renowned for illustrating historical reference books for children and young adults.

Contents

INTRODUCTION

The Pharaohs ruled Egypt for about 3,000 years. They were one of the most successful and long-lasting lines of Kings ever known. But to be a Pharaoh was much more than merely being King. When the Pharaoh wore the sacred royal regalia and sat on his throne, the spirit of Horus, god of both Kings and the sky, was thought to enter him. He became god-on-earth. Ancient Egyptians also believed the Pharaoh was descended from Re the sun god, and that Re's blood ran in his veins.

Naturally, the Pharaoh was immensely powerful. He actually owned the land of Egypt. He was responsible for running the country, for its foreign policy, its trade and for the safety and prosperity of his subjects. He was commander of the army and navy, and head of the cults of all the gods and goddesses of Egypt. He made the laws and gave out punishments.

His influence with the gods was believed to control the weather, and the River Nile, make the crops grow and the flocks and herds of animals increase.
It was also his job to see that his subjects were cared for in the Next World.

The only real check on the Pharaoh's actions was the will of the gods. He was expected to keep the world in the perfect state which the gods had originally created.

6

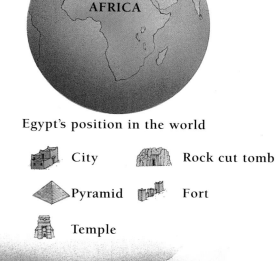

AFRICA

Egypt's position in the world

City   Rock cut tomb

Pyramid   Fort

Temple

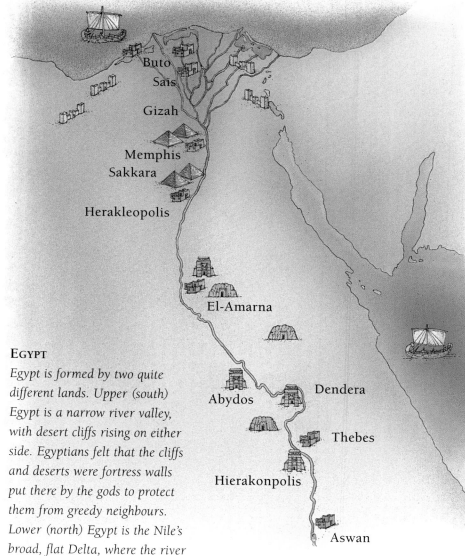

Buto
Saïs
Gizah
Memphis
Sakkara
Herakleopolis
El-Amarna

EGYPT

Egypt is formed by two quite different lands. Upper (south) Egypt is a narrow river valley, with desert cliffs rising on either side. Egyptians felt that the cliffs and deserts were fortress walls put there by the gods to protect them from greedy neighbours. Lower (north) Egypt is the Nile's broad, flat Delta, where the river flows to the sea through several channels.

Abydos   Dendera

Thebes

Hierakonpolis

Aswan

The Double Crown symbolized a
united Egypt, consisting of the White
Crown of Upper Egypt and the Red
Crown of Lower Egypt.

*The word 'Pharaoh' comes from two ancient
Egyptian words* per o, *meaning 'Great House' or
Palace. It was not considered respectful to speak
of the King as a person, so people said 'The
Palace' did this or ordered that. In the New
Kingdom, 'Pharaoh' was sometimes used as if it
were the King's title. This term was used in the
Bible, which is why we use it today.*

The flail symbolized
the punishment the
King would give to
wrong-doers and
enemies.

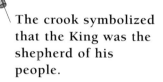

False
beard

The crook symbolized
that the King was the
shepherd of his
people.

THE HORUS PENDANT

*Horus was often depicted as a soaring
falcon. His eyes were the sun and moon
and his feathers were the clouds.*

Gold necklaces set
with semi-precious
stones.

7

THE KING AND HORUS

*This statue shows the special relationship
between Horus and the King. The King is
seated on his throne and Horus, as a
falcon, perches on his shoulder. He both
guards the King and becomes part of him.*

Pleated skirt of
finest linen, with
a belt of gilded
leather and
jewels.

The bull's tail showed
that the King had the
strength of a wild bull.

THE KING'S REGALIA

*The King's regalia consisted of
the Double Crown, a crook and
flail, a false beard and a bull's
tail. Naturally, the King always
had the best of everything –
gold and jewels, the finest linen
and the softest leather.*

Gilded leather sandals

HISTORY OF EGYPT

Thousands of years ago, the Sahara was a well-watered, grassy plain. People roamed across it in search of wild animals, plants, nuts and fruits. Slowly, the climate changed and the Sahara became a desert. Some people trekked east in search of water and found the River Nile.

c.5000 – 3100 BC
THE PREDYNASTIC PERIOD

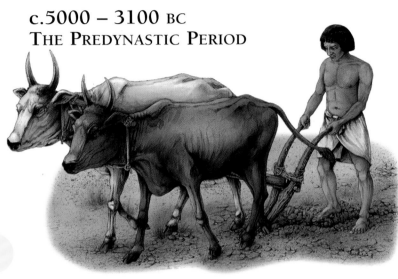

• By 5000 BC, farmers had settled on the fertile land beside the Nile. They dug canals and ditches to store and control the Nile's annual floodwaters.
• Cloth and pottery were made.
• By the end of this period, artefacts were made in copper and gold.
• Construction of large mud-brick buildings.
• Invention of picture writing.
• Villages were united to form two kingdoms – Upper Egypt in the south (the valley), with its capital at Hierakonpolis, and Lower Egypt in the north (the Delta) with Buto as its capital.

THE RULE OF THE PHARAOHS

The Pharaohs ruled Egypt for over 3,000 years. Egyptologists have identified five long prosperous periods and short, unsettled periods. The long periods are known as the Archaic, Old, Middle and New Kingdoms ('kingdom' here means a length of time) and the Late Period. The unsettled times are called the Intermediate Periods. Pharaohs are grouped by Dynasties – rulers from related families.

c.3100 – 2686 BC
THE ARCHAIC PERIOD

• Menes, King of Upper Egypt, conquered Lower Egypt and united the Two Lands.
• A new capital was built at Memphis, on the border between the Two Lands. United Egypt was well-organized and grew rich.
• Huge mud-brick tombs, now known as mastabas, were built for the kings at Abydos and Sakkara.

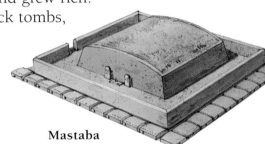

Mastaba

SECOND DYNASTY C.2890 – 2686 BC
• Unrest between the north and south.
• Peace and unity were restored by King Khasekhemwy.

c.2686 – 2181 BC
THE OLD KINGDOM

THIRD DYNASTY C. 2686 - 2613 BC
• Peace and prosperity. Art, literature, medicine, architecture and engineering flourished.

• The first step pyramid was built for King Zoser.

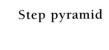

Step pyramid

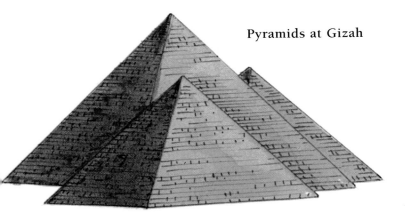

Pyramids at Gizah

FOURTH DYNASTY c.2613 – 2494 BC
• Straight-sided pyramids were built at Sakkara and Gizah. The largest belonged to King Khufu.
• Timber trade with the city of Byblos.
• Copper and turquoise trade with Sinai.
• A trading post was established at Buhen, in Nubia.
• Incense trade with Punt (Somalia).
• Fighting with Libyans, Nubians and eastern nomads.

Re

FIFTH DYNASTY c.2494 – 2345 BC
• The sun god Re became the most important deity. Kings built temples to honor him and took the title 'Son of Re'.
• The size of pyramids declined.

SIXTH DYNASTY c.2345 – 2181 BC
• Problems arose both in Egypt and abroad.
• At the end of the Dynasty, the government collapsed into chaos, as the Kings lost influence and Nomarchs (district governors) became more powerful.

C.2181 – 2025 BC
THE FIRST INTERMEDIATE PERIOD
• Two Dynasties of weak kings with short reigns.
• The Nomarchs of Herakleopolis won control of much of the country and ruled as kings of the Ninth and Tenth Dynasties. The Nomarchs of Thebes opposed them in the south.

C.2025 – 1700 BC
THE MIDDLE KINGDOM
ELEVENTH DYNASTY c.2025 – 1985 BC
• Mentuhotep, ruler of Thebes, conquered the north, re-united Egypt and restored peace, prosperity and strong government.
• Thebes became the capital.

TWELFTH DYNASTY c.1985 – 1795 BC
• Mentuhotep's family was replaced by a new Dynasty, whose kings were all called Amenemhat or Senusret.
• The capital moved to It-Towy, near Memphis.

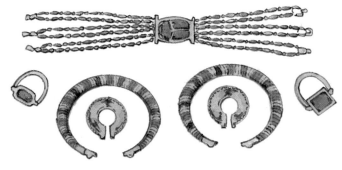

Jewellery

• Great age of achievement in arts, crafts and literature.
• Trade bought great wealth to Egypt again.
• Kings opened up the Fayum oasis and were buried around it in pyramids.
• Northern Nubia was conquered.
• A chain of forts was built to protect the new (or Nubian) frontier.
• King Senusret III fought the warrior Kushites in south Nubia.
• A chain of forts was built to protect the eastern frontier.
• Male line of kings died out with Amenemhat IV. His sister, Sobekneferu, reigned as 'King'.

THIRTEENTH DYNASTY
c.1795 – 1700 BC
• Rapid turnover of Kings.
• Royal power weakened and Nubia was lost.

c.1700 – 1550 BC
THE SECOND INTERMEDIATE PERIOD
FOURTEENTH TO SEVENTEENTH DYNASTIES
- The Hyksos overran Egypt from the east, using horse-drawn chariots, previously unknown in Egypt.
- The Hyksos ruled the Delta from their capital, Avaris. Egyptian lords ruled as their allies in the central part of the country. The independent south paid tribute to the Hyksos.
- After 100 years of conquest, there was a revolt against the Hyksos, led by a prince of Thebes.

c.1550 – 1069 BC
THE NEW KINGDOM
EIGHTEENTH DYNASTY C. 1550 - 1295 BC
- The Hyksos were expelled by King Ahmose.
- Warrior Kings, Amenhotep I and II and Tuthmosis I, began the conquest of a vast empire.

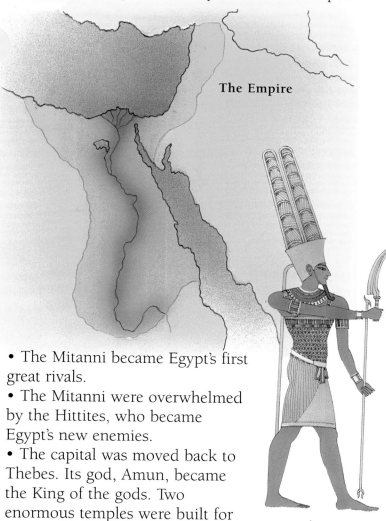

The Empire

- The Mitanni became Egypt's first great rivals.
- The Mitanni were overwhelmed by the Hittites, who became Egypt's new enemies.
- The capital was moved back to Thebes. Its god, Amun, became the King of the gods. Two enormous temples were built for him on the east bank.

Amun

Tutankhamun

- New Kingdom Kings were buried in tombs cut into the cliffs of the Valley of the Kings on the west bank at Thebes. Only the tomb of the boy-King, Tutankhamun, escaped the later tomb robberies.
- Tribute and trade made Egypt unbelievably rich.
- After the death of her husband, Queen Hatshepsut was accepted as King.
- Tuthmosis III, her successor, won much of Egypt's empire.
- During the reign of King Akhenaten, worship of all gods except Aten, symbolized by the sun's disc, was banned.
- Queen Nefertiti, Akhenaten's wife became a 'King' towards the end of Akhenaten's reign and ruled by his side.

Queen Nefertiti

- Most of the eastern empire was lost to the Hittites.

NINETEETH DYNASTY C.1295 – 1186 BC
- Part of the lost empire was won back by Seti I and Ramesses II.
- Reign of Ramesses II, 'The Great'.
- Squabbles among the descendants of Ramesses II over who should succeed him.

Ramesses II

- Queen Tawosret was the last 'King' of the Dynasty.

TWENTIETH DYNASTY C.1186 – 1069 BC
- Sea Peoples, who had wiped out the Hittite empire, threatened Egypt's independence, but were defeated by Ramesses III.
- Decline of Egypt. Price rises, tomb robberies, strikes, conspiracies, dishonest officials and civil war weakened the country.
- The eastern half of the empire was lost entirely.

c.1069 – 664 BC
THE THIRD INTERMEDIATE PERIOD
TWENTY FIRST DYNASTY c.1069 –- 945 BC
• The throne was seized by a family of top officials.
• Egypt was ruled from a new capital, Tanis, in the Delta.
• The royal family was buried in tombs under a temple courtyard in Tanis.
• Egypt was disadvantaged by having no deposits of iron, the metal now used by its enemies to make weapons and tools.

TWENTY-SECOND TO TWENTY-FOURTH DYNASTY c.945 –- 715 BC
• Kings of these Dynasties were descended from Libyan soldiers who had previously served in the Egyptian army.
• Shesonq I invaded the Kingdom of Judah and carried off treasures from the Temple and palace at Jerusalem.

Coffin of Shesonq II

• The royal family was split by rival princes competing for the throne. At one time, five rival rulers divided Egypt between them.

TWENTY-FIFTH DYNASTY c.715 – 664 BC
• Egypt was invaded by King Piankhy of Nubia, who established a new Dynasty.
• The Assyrians attacked Egypt. Thebes was sacked and the Nubians were driven out.

Assyrian soldier

c.664 – 332 BC
THE LATE PERIOD
TWENTY-SIXTH – THIRTIETH DYNASTIES
• Egypt's greatness was restored by the kings of the Twenty-sixth Dynasty. The Assyrians were driven out.
• A new capital was established at the ancient Delta city of Saïs.
• Ancient styles and cults were revived. Studies and excavations of old temples, tombs and texts.
• Egypt was conquered twice by Persians (during the Twenty-seventh and Thirty-first Dynasties).

c.332 – 30 BC
PTOLEMAIC PERIOD
(including Alexander's occupation)
• Alexander the Great, King of Macedonia (Greece) was regarded as a hero for driving out the much loathed Persians.
• After Alexander's death, Egypt was seized by one of his generals, Ptolemy, who ruled from the newly-built city of Alexandria.
• After initial prosperity under these foreign Pharaohs, Egypt

Ptolemy I

became neglected when bitter power struggles broke out.
• Egypt flourished again under the rule of Queen Cleopatra VII, but she supported Mark Anthony in the civil wars raging in Rome. After his defeat they both committed suicide.

• Egypt became part of the Roman Empire. The Roman emperors' title, *Kings of Upper and Lower Egypt*, was an empty one. They were interested only in Egyptian wheat to feed Rome's teeming masses. Egypt's true kings, the Pharaohs, were gone and with them went her greatness and independence.

Cleopatra VII

THE RIVER NILE

BOATS ON THE NILE

Early Egyptian boats were made of reed bundles. These were used for travelling on the river throughout Ancient Egyptian times. Once the Egyptians learned how to build wooden boats, they used wood for all large boats, such as warships and trading vessels, for both sea and river travel. The most magnificent of all was the King's state barge. Once, some traitors tried to capture the royal barge of King Ramesses III and kill him.

It hardly ever rains in Egypt, so the Nile was the only source of water to meet all the needs of people, animals and crops. In ancient times, every year, from mid-July until mid-October, the Nile spilled over its banks, flooding the flat lands of the river valley and the Delta. The floods carried black mud on to the fields and made them very fertile. Throughout the year, the river teemed with fish. Along its banks were dense reed beds. The reeds were used to make roofs, mats, paper, baskets, furniture, sandals and small boats. The Nile itself was Egypt's major highway. It was far easier and quicker to carry people and heavy goods by water than over the desert sands or across muddy fields.

FACT AND FICTION

The River Nile flows from south to north. When the Egyptians encountered the River Euphrates, which flows from north to south, they were so amazed that they called it the 'topsy-turvy' river.

Journeys by boat were so essential to the Egyptians that they believed the sun god Re travelled across the sky in a boat every day. They also believed that they had to cross a river to reach the Next World.

THE GOD OF THE NILE

Hapi, the god of the Nile, was depicted carrying the river's gifts, such as papyrus, vegetables, fruits and wild fowl. It was the King's task to persuade Hapi to make the Nile flood on time and to the right height.

13

NILOMETERS

The King needed to know the flood level, so that he could plan to change taxes or meet a threatened famine. Stone buildings, called Nilometers, had steps down to the river and marks on the wall which measured how far the river was rising above its normal level.

HIPPO HUNTING

Fishing and trapping birds earned some peasants a living, but for Kings and nobles these were sports. The most dangerous river sport was harpooning hippos. There was also a ceremony in which the King ritually killed a hippo. A male hippo represented evil. By harpooning one, the King demonstrated that he could protect his people from evil.

THE FERTILE LAND

14

PLOUGHING AND SOWING

Ploughing with oxen began as soon as the floods went down. The seed was scattered by hand and sheep were driven over the fields to trample it into the soft, damp earth. Each farmer's fields were marked by heavy boundary stones. Villages were built above the flood level.

The Egyptians called the area where they grew crops the 'Black Land', because of the black mud that settled there after the flood. Farming was the main source of Egypt's wealth. In theory, the King owned all the land but, in practice, he let people and temples farm parcels of land, in return for taxes. From early in their history, the Egyptians dug storage lakes to store the floodwater. They cut a network of canals to channel water for the crops. Organizing the irrigation system was the King's responsibility. After the harvest, he ordered the cleaning and repair of canals and decided if any new ones were needed. One person from every household might be ordered to join this vital work.

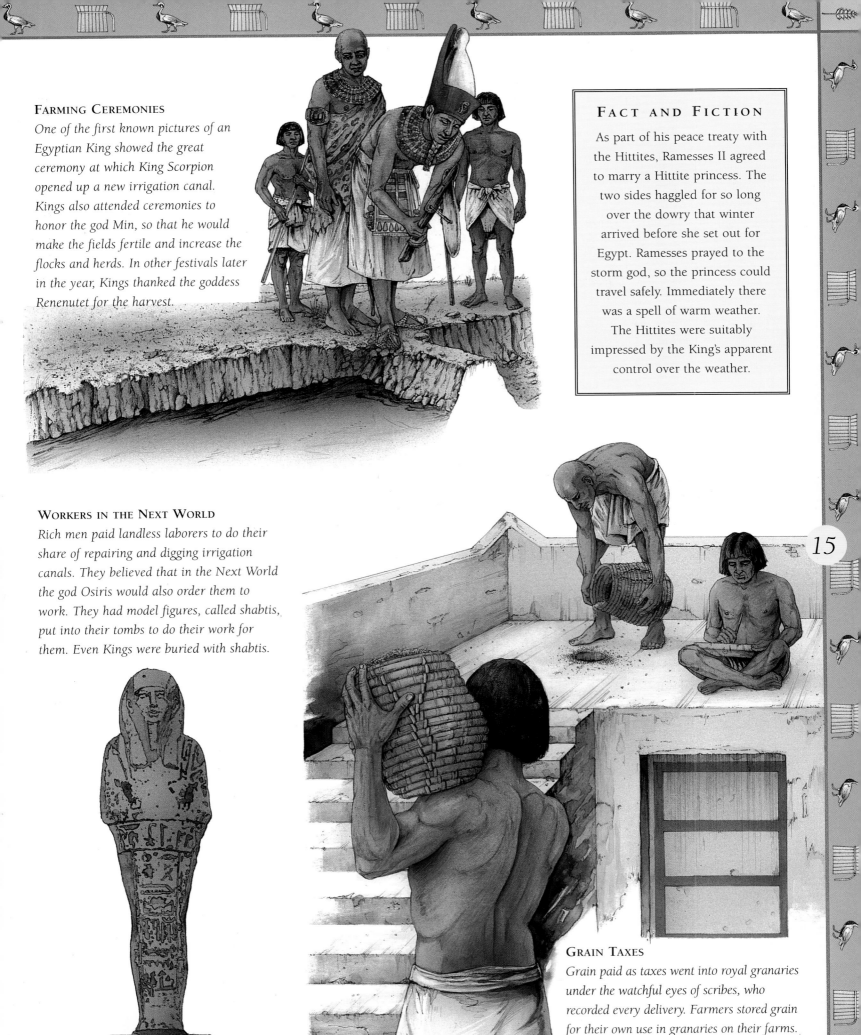

FARMING CEREMONIES

One of the first known pictures of an Egyptian King showed the great ceremony at which King Scorpion opened up a new irrigation canal. Kings also attended ceremonies to honor the god Min, so that he would make the fields fertile and increase the flocks and herds. In other festivals later in the year, Kings thanked the goddess Renenutet for the harvest.

FACT AND FICTION

As part of his peace treaty with the Hittites, Ramesses II agreed to marry a Hittite princess. The two sides haggled for so long over the dowry that winter arrived before she set out for Egypt. Ramesses prayed to the storm god, so the princess could travel safely. Immediately there was a spell of warm weather. The Hittites were suitably impressed by the King's apparent control over the weather.

WORKERS IN THE NEXT WORLD

Rich men paid landless laborers to do their share of repairing and digging irrigation canals. They believed that in the Next World the god Osiris would also order them to work. They had model figures, called shabtis, put into their tombs to do their work for them. Even Kings were buried with shabtis.

15

GRAIN TAXES

Grain paid as taxes went into royal granaries under the watchful eyes of scribes, who recorded every delivery. Farmers stored grain for their own use in granaries on their farms.

THE DESERT

16

HUNTING IN THE DESERT

Before the horse was introduced into Egypt, hunting was done on foot, and animals were driven into large, netted enclosures. During the New Kingdom, the use of horse-drawn chariots made hunting for lions, gazelles, ostriches, jackals, foxes and hares much easier.

Apart from the Black Land, the rest of Egypt was desert, which the Egyptians called the 'Red Land'. This was partly because of its color, but also because it was seen as a place of danger, home of the evil, red-headed god Set. Kings and nobles hunted there and trading expeditions plodded between oases with goods on donkeys. The Red Land provided stone for building temples and tombs and for carving statues. It was rich in semi-precious stones and metals, such as copper and gold. Only the King could order stone quarrying and metal mining. As a special favor, he might allow nobles or a temple to quarry the stone they needed.

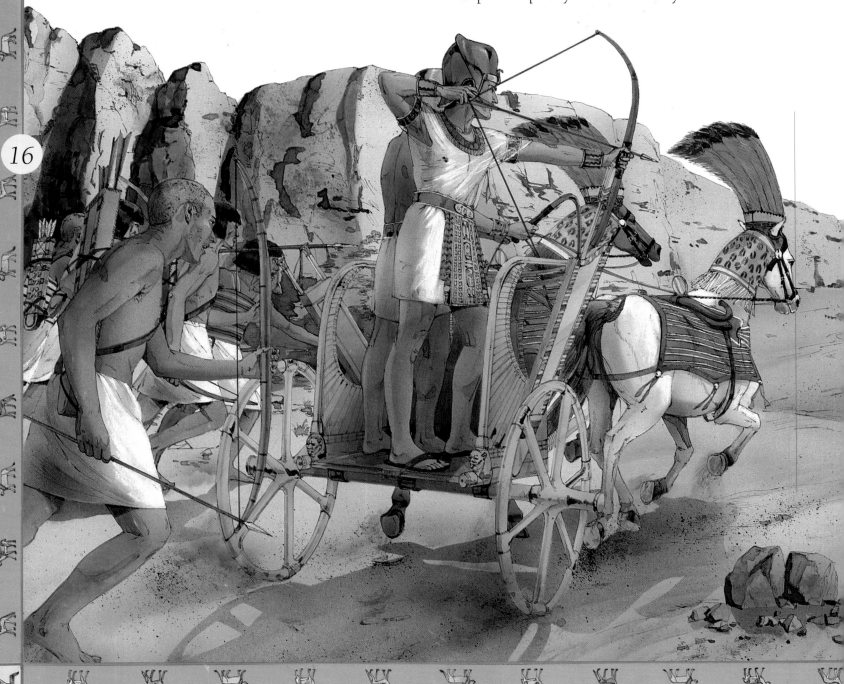

QUARRYING FOR STONE

To make stone blocks, men started by carving holes in the rock face. They knocked wooden wedges into these holes and poured water over them. As the wedges swelled, they split the blocks away from the rock face. The blocks were roughly shaped with chisels and mallets. They were then transported on sledges, pulled by teams of men, to the sites of temples and tombs. Here they were shaped precisely to fit.

GLITTERING GOLD

Gold for the most expensive jewellery came from the eastern deserts of Egypt and Nubia. The Nubian mines were especially rich, so the Egyptians benefited in the Middle and New Kingdoms, particularly when Nubia was part of their Empire.

THE KING SHOWS HIS BRAVERY

Hunting was an exciting sport, but it also showed the people how brave and fit their king was. Amenhotep III had dozens of special amulets (charms worn as protection against evil) made in the shape of scarab beetles. Inscriptions on the base of these proudly recorded how, in the first ten years of his reign, he had killed one hundred and two very fierce lions.

FACT AND FICTION

One day, a Prince on a hunting trip in the desert took a rest from the mid-day heat in the shadow of the Sphinx at Gizah. In those days, the Sphinx was covered by sand up to its neck. It appeared to the Prince in a dream and promised to make him King if he had the sand cleared away. The Prince did as he was asked and the Sphinx kept its bargain. The Prince eventually became King Tuthmosis IV, after all his elder brothers died before him.

MA'AT

Egyptians believed that the gods created a perfect world. All forces were in perfect balance and harmony, so that night, dark and evil could not overcome day, light and the good, and the desert could not swallow up the Black Land. The King's job was to rule wisely to preserve that balance, which was represented by this goddess, Ma'at.

Ma'at

18

The Egyptians believed that the first rulers of Egypt were the gods themselves. The last god to rule was Horus. He returned to heaven, but sent his spirit to earth. When his spirit entered the body of the mortal King, he became god on earth. This set the King apart, even from other members of his family.

Kings also claimed to be descended from the sun god Re. The first three Kings of the Fifth Dynasty were said to be Re's sons by a beautiful mortal woman. All Kings after them were thought to have divine blood.

RE
sun god

SHU
god of air

TEFNUT
goddess of moisture

GEB
god of the earth

NUT
goddess of the sky

ISIS
goddess of magic

THE GODS' FAMILY TREE
In the beginning there was only water. The first god, Atum, who lived in the water, created a mound, the first land, that rose out of it. Re appeared on the mound and created the other gods and goddesses, and then the world.

OSIRIS
ruler of the Next World

NEPHTHYS
protector of the dead

SET
god of the desert, chaos and evil

HORUS
god of the sky

HATHOR
mother goddess, also goddess of the sky, love, joy and death

ANUBIS
god of embalming

THE TEMPLE

The Egyptians believed that their gods and goddesses were so glorious and powerful that no ordinary person could approach them. The King, part god himself, provided a living link between the gods and people. A person with a special plea (such as wanting a baby) would pray to one of the colossal statues of the King at a temple gate. People hoped that his spirit would ask his divine relatives to grant the request.

FACT AND FICTION

At a ceremony, King Neferirkare's walking stick slipped and hit Rawer, a priest. The poor man was terrified. He regarded the god-King with such awe, that he was convinced he was going to die. The King assured him that it was an accident. This was the greatest moment of Rawer's career. He recorded the story in his tomb.

BECOMING A KING

The King chose which of his sons (usually the Queen's eldest) was to rule after him, and presented him to the court as the heir. When the old King died, the new King conducted the funeral which, in Egyptian eyes, showed that he was the accepted heir. It was the coronation that turned the prince into a god-King. The Egyptians believed that all the gods and goddesses and the ancestors (spirits of past Kings) were present and agreed that the new King was the rightful successor. In a series of rituals, he took possession of Egypt as his inheritance. Finally, as the double crown and the crook and flail (the symbols of kingship that had once belonged to Horus) were presented to the King, the god's spirit entered him.

THE FIRST DAY OF A NEW REIGN

The death of a King was a calamity. Evil was, for a while, triumphant. But the next morning, just as Re had appeared on the first mound of land on the day of Creation, so the new King, on the first day of his reign, appeared dazzling and glorious on a dais. The dais represented the mound. He sat down on a throne, which represented the goddess Isis. The name Isis and the word for throne are the same in hieroglyphics. So by sitting on his throne, the King was considered to have been reborn as Isis's son, Horus, the true ruler of Egypt.

20

THE KING'S REGALIA

THE BLUE CROWN

The Blue Crown was the King's helmet. It appeared in the Second Intermediate Period and was much favoured by New Kingdom Kings.

THE DIADEM

This was worn by itself on less formal occasions or combined with the nemes head-dress.

THE NEMES

Also called the sphinx head-dress, the nemes was a blue striped head-cloth, worn on less formal occasions.

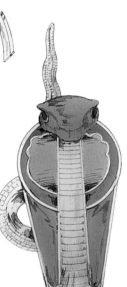

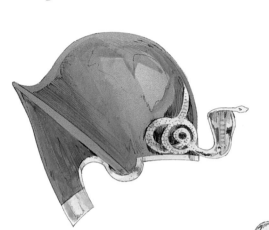

THE ATEF CROWN

This was the crown of Osiris. It is difficult to believe that a King would wear this for any length of time. However, he is shown wearing it at some religious ceremonies.

THE URAEUS

People believed that, on the King's forehead, sat the uraeus, a snake called 'Great of Magic', that spat fire at his enemies.

THE SEKHEM SCEPTRE

This symbol of royal power was carried at various ceremonies.

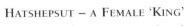

HATSHEPSUT – A FEMALE 'KING'

The Kings of Egypt were male. They had to be – they were god on earth. Even so, Egypt was ruled by at least half a dozen women, but they all had to take the title of King. The most famous female 'King' was Hatshepsut, heiress of a long line of Kings and Queens. She ruled very successfully for about 20 years, fighting on campaigns, rebuilding temples ruined by the Hyksos and promoting Egypt's trade. She is often depicted wearing a beard.

THE ROYAL FAMILY

A King normally had one Queen (her title was the 'Great Royal Wife'), who was often his sister or half-sister. This was quite acceptable to the Egyptians, because it meant that she had the blood of the sun god in her veins to pass on to her children. Also, when King of Egypt, the god Osiris had married his sister Isis, who became Egypt's Queen. The Crown Prince, the King's chosen heir, was usually the Queen's son. If she had no sons, the King chose a son of one of his minor wives. Kings married as many wives of lesser rank as they wanted. Among these wives were often foreign princesses, whose marriages helped to cement friendships between their countries and Egypt.

Hathor's crown

Vulture head-dress of the goddess Mut

Sceptre with a lilyflower handle

Feathered dress of a goddess

A NEW KINGDOM QUEEN

This Queen is wearing her ceremonial costume. In the New Kingdom, it was believed that the spirit of the goddess Hathor could enter a Queen, so that she became a goddess on earth. This belief made a Queen far more powerful than she had ever been before.

THE GOD AMUN

New Kingdom Queens were also called 'Wife of God', in reference to Amun, King of the gods. The Egyptians believed that sometimes Amun's spirit came to earth and entered the King's body. A child born to the Queen was therefore the son of both her husbands - the god and the King. It was believed that Amun clearly intended that such a son was destined to be the next King.

CROWN PRINCE AND PRINCESS

The Crown Prince had his own official palace at Memphis and was appointed the High Priest of the god Ptah at Memphis. He was also a top army officer and a 'Fan-bearer of the Right Hand' (a top courtier). Both the Crown Prince and his sister, his future wife and Queen, had the side-lock of youth hairstyle, which all children wore.

Diadem with uraeus

Gazelle-head diadem

JEWELLERY TO SHOW ROYAL RANK

The symbols on royal diadems were a sign of rank. Only a member of the royal family could wear a diadem with the uraeus (see page 21) on the front. Lesser wives, at least in the New Kingdom, wore gazelle heads on the front of their diadems.

23

QUEEN TIY

Tiy was probably 5 years old when she married the King, 10-year-old Amenhotep III. Later, she became very powerful, playing an active part in decisions and government. Amenhotep had hundreds of minor wives, but none could compete with Tiy.

ROYAL EDUCATION

All princes and princesses were carefully educated as no-one knew which ones might suddenly be called upon to become King or Queen. Training in all weapons was a vital skill for princes.

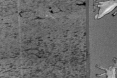

ROYAL PALACES

The King's palace was built of sun-dried mud bricks, with stone door frames and pillars. The inside was magnificent, glowing with paintings, glazed tiles and gold leaf. The elegant furniture was made of rare woods, decorated with gold, ivory and precious stones. The palace was not one building but several. The King received ambassadors and held ceremonies in the official palace with its courtyards and huge columned halls leading to a throne room. The King, Queen and Crown Prince all had separate palaces for their living quarters.

A COURTIER AND HIS WIFE

This is a 'Fan-bearer of the Right Hand', a top ranking courtier. He also ran the royal household. His wife is a Chantress (Priestess) of Amun and keeper of the Royal Wigs. A position like this was considered a great honor.

A PALACE PROCESSION

The King was considered far too holy to walk to temple festivals, so servants carried him on a chair made of ebony, inlaid with gold, ivory and jewels. The Queen and the rest of the royal family followed on in their own carrying chairs.

24

THE PALACE

As well as palaces for the Royal family, there were apartments for lesser wives and their children, shady gardens with pools and even a royal zoo. Courtiers who ran the royal estates and palaces had their own living quarters, as did the palace servants and entertainers. There were also offices and homes for court officials, craft workshops, kitchens and stables.

THE WINDOW OF APPEARANCES

A highly favoured courtier or official and his wife might be made 'People of the Gold'. The King and Queen stood at their 'Window of Appearances' and showered gold necklaces down on the lucky pair to honor them. The other courtiers cheered wildly – doubtless hoping their own turn would come soon.

GOVERNING EGYPT

It was hard work being King of Egypt – there was so much to do! Because the King owned all of Egypt, was the head of absolutely everything and made every decision, it was essential for good government that he was strong, clever and hard-working. If he was weak, officials grew lazy or corrupt, irrigation canals were not repaired, causing food shortages, law and order broke down and Egypt suffered. Similarly, if several Kings had short reigns, one after the other, officials and nobles could become too powerful. This could lead to unrest, even to civil war and a new royal family coming to power. Neighboring countries, envious of Egypt's riches, often took advantage of a weak King to invade.

THE PEOPLE IN CHARGE

The King had two sets of ministers and civil servants – one each for Upper and Lower Egypt. The two chief ministers were called Viziers, then came heads of government departments and hundreds of officials. Everything was recorded by scribes (official writers). Clever and ambitious scribes could reach positions of great power in the government.

COURTS AND APPEALS

Egyptians believed their legal system was fair and honest. Ordinary cases were tried by local courts with local judges. Appeals went to higher courts, such as the District or Vizier's courts, which also tried more serious cases. Some appeals were heard by the King himself.

THE MEDJAY ON PATROL

To help him keep the peace, guard the tombs and catch criminals, the King had the Medjay – a sort of police force. Originally the King hired Nubian soldiers, but, later, Egyptians also joined the Medjay. Punishments varied with the crime. These included warnings, fines, hard labor, beatings, mutilation, exile and, for the most serious crimes, such as tomb robbery, death.

FACT AND FICTION

The King had five titles. The first three say that he was Horus, protected by Nekhbet (the vulture goddess) and Wadjet (the cobra goddess). His main titles were 'The King of Upper and Lower Egypt' (with the name he took when he became King) and 'The Son of Re' (followed by his personal name).

VICEROYS AND PRINCES RULE

Nubia and Kush (the southern part of the empire) adopted the Egyptian way of life and religion. They were ruled by a Viceroy (in place of a Vizier), with help from Egyptian officials and local chiefs. People of the eastern empire kept their own way of life and were ruled by their own princes, overseen by Egyptian officials.

THE KING'S TAXES

ALL PULL TOGETHER

During the Nile flood, when no-one could work in the fields, every household could be ordered to send one person to do labor tax. These people worked for the King on a royal building project, or in quarries or mines. They were cared for and paid in goods by the King. Although cutting and shaping of stone was done by skilled masons, hauling was one of the unskilled jobs for those doing labor tax.

Everyone in Egypt had to pay taxes to the King. Before coins were invented (just before 600 BC), people paid taxes in goods and labor. Farmers paid in wheat and barley after the harvest. How much they paid depended upon the height of the Nile flood and how good the resulting harvest was. Fishermen and bird catchers probably paid with part of their catch over the whole year. Craftsmen and women paid with the things that they made. With these taxes, the King paid his officials, soldiers, sailors and craftsmen. He housed and fed his slaves and also fed widows and orphans of some of the men who had been on his service. The surplus was traded abroad for essential goods that Egypt lacked, as well as for luxury goods.

BUYING BY BARTER

Money did not exist, so people had to barter – pay for their goods by giving other goods in exchange. Since it could be difficult to work out the relative value of things, Egyptians quoted prices as weights, called 'deben', which were made of copper or silver. They had nearly, but not quite, invented money.

MEASURED FOR TAX

Royal taxmen measured the farmers' growing crops to work out how much each one should pay in taxes. One text details the misery of farmers if locusts or birds ate their crops or hippos flattened them after the tax had been set.

29

ALL FOR THE KING

The best craftsmen worked for the King, making both luxury objects, such as jewellery, or everyday ones, such as shoes, jars or clothes. All the King's palaces, workshops, storerooms and fortresses were made of mud bricks, that had been baked hard in the sun. Countless millions were made every year. The outer wall of one fortress alone was built with over 8,600,000 bricks!

TEMPLES & PRIESTS

Egyptians believed that temples were the homes of their gods and goddesses on earth. It was the King's responsibility to build temples and make them so beautiful that the gods would happily come to earth and bless the land. He also gave the temples land to support them and, after a successful campaign, gave them a share of the booty and prisoners. The King was thought to have inherited Egypt from the gods, Re, Osiris and Horus, just as a peasant would inherit a farm from his father. He was therefore responsible for making offerings to all his divine relatives every day, just as an Egyptian son made offerings to his dead parents. The King appointed priests, as his deputies, to help him. He only conducted the rituals at the most important festivals.

AKHENATEN
King Amenhotep IV believed that Aten, an ancient sun god, was the only god. To honor this god, the King changed his name to Akhenaten and banned the worship of all the other gods and goddesses. This was very unpopular.

THE ROLE OF THE PRIESTS
There were two types of priest. Those called 'the god's servant' conducted rituals and made offerings. A High Priest presided over them. The rest, known as 'the pure ones' played minor roles, such as carrying the god's statue in its divine boat at festivals. Priestesses were responsible for singing the words of the rituals.

SPEAKING STATUES

Just as Horus's spirit was thought to enter the King, so the spirits of the gods and goddesses were thought to enter their statues. The King or the priests could ask questions which a god or goddess answered through a statue. This was how the gods approved the King's ideas or ordered him to do something. A god might make a statue move or speak. If a statue was being carried, it might suddenly become so heavy that the bearers sank to their knees.

THE FESTIVAL OF THE TAIL

When he had reigned for 30 years, the King held a jubilee, called the heb sed. *This was the 'festival of the tail', meaning the bull's tail that was part of the King's regalia. Rituals conducted by the* priests revitalised the King's strength, so he could continue ruling. The King demonstrated his renewed vigor by running between two markers. The King carried a papyrus roll of the title deeds to Egypt, which proved that he owned the whole country.

THE EGYPTIAN ARMY

TUTHMOSIS III
Tuthmosis III was the greatest of Egypt's warrior Pharaohs. He led 17 (and probably four more) campaigns against the Nubians, Canaanites and Mitanni. The empire reached its widest extent during his reign.

In the Old and Middle Kingdoms, the King had a bodyguard and a small army. In emergencies, he called up all adult male Egyptians, who were given basic training. He also hired mercenaries. The soldiers fought on foot, with only a shield for protection. They fought successfully against the Nubians, Libyans and the Bedouin in Sinai and South Canaan. Tomb paintings show them capturing cities using battering rams and scaling ladders. When the Hyksos conquered Egypt with horse-drawn chariots, this revolutionized warfare. The Egyptians became expert charioteers too and planned battles using chariots to their best advantage. The New Kingdom army was a large, well-trained mixture of infantry (foot soldiers) and chariots. These soldiers wore helmets and armor. They were divided into companies, each with its own battle standard.

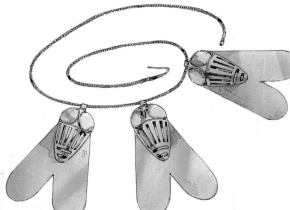

GOLDEN FLIES
The Kings awarded golden flies, which were worn as necklaces, as medals for bravery. This one belonged to Queen Ah-hotep, who led an army into battle, whilst acting as Regent for her young son.

BATTLES AGAINST THE SEA PEOPLES
There were very few naval battles. The most important one took place when Ramesses III saved Egypt from being conquered by the Sea Peoples (from Greece and Western Turkey). Ramesses fought them on both land and sea. He won great victories, but it needed all his soldiers, sailors and reserves to succeed.

SOLDIERS

Egyptian and mercenary foot soldiers in the Middle Kingdom were armed with spears, battle axes, daggers, maces and bows and arrows. Their large shields were made of wood and leather.

Besides their normal weapons, New Kingdom soldiers copied the Hyksos' bow, which was much stronger and shot further. Some also copied the Hyksos' curved swords for hand-to-hand fighting. They wore a leather and metal tunic for body protection and helmets.

Middle Kingdom
soldier

Nubian mercenary in
the Middle Kingdom

New Kingdom standard
bearer and archer

COUNTING HANDS

When an Egyptian soldier killed an enemy, he cut off the dead man's right hand. After a battle, the hands were counted to find out how many enemies had been slain. This helped the work of the army scribes, who kept detailed records of each campaign for the King.

WARRIOR KINGS

FORTRESSES ON THE FRONTIERS

To help protect their frontiers, the Kings of the Twelfth Dynasty built several mud-brick fortresses around the 2nd Cataract and another chain across their eastern frontier. Ramesses II built another string of forts across the western Delta to keep out the Libyans. These had huge walls, towers and deep ditches.

It was the duty of the King, laid upon him by the gods at the time of Creation, to protect Egypt from its enemies. In the Predynastic and Archaic Periods, Kings probably led their troops into battle. However, during the Old Kingdom, the King was considered too holy to take part in battles. Generals took charge instead. In the Middle Kingdom, Kings led their troops once more. During the New Kingdom, Egypt was at the height of its power and conquered a vast empire. Now Kings were expected to be heroes, leading their armies to glory. The god Amun told the King whom and when to fight. The Kings informed the gods and the people of their victories on the outside walls of temples, and rewarded their soldiers with medals, gold, slaves and land.

THE NINE ENEMIES OF EGYPT

In the Old Kingdom, the Egyptians identified nine foreign peoples as their enemies. The number of enemies stayed the same but old enemies were dropped and new ones were added. Nubians, Libyans and the Bedouin of the Eastern Desert were the main foes in the Middle Kingdom. As the Egyptians expanded their empire, the people of Kush (modern Sudan) and Canaan were added to their list of enemies. In the New Kingdom, the Egyptians' greatest imperial rivals were the Mitanni and the Hittites.

Libyan

Kushite

Mitannian warrior

THE KING RIDES INTO BATTLE

A New Kingdom King was expected to be the bravest in battle, the most skilled charioteer, the most successful huntsman and the most brilliant and cunning general. Enthusiastic scribes described him as a lion savaging his enemies. Sometimes he is shown as a sphinx, trampling on fallen foes. Ramesses II had a real lion who went into battle by his side. The King had a large bodyguard to protect him in battle. It would have been a catastrophe if the King was killed.

FACT AND FICTION

If Kings ever lost a battle, they ignored the fact. They knew that their gods intended Egypt to triumph in the end, so they omitted to mention any set-backs. Ramesses II claimed to have won an overwhelming victory at Kadesh in Canaan. In reality, it is known that, at best, the battle was a draw.

EXECUTION BY BATTLE MACE

In Egyptian eyes, people who opposed them were rebels worthy only of death. Throughout Egyptian history, artists depicted scenes of Kings executing rebel leaders. They held them tightly by the hair and smashed their skulls with a battle mace.

TRADE & TRIBUTE

Ivory

Ebony

Giraffe

Slaves

Leopard

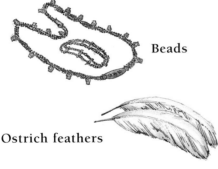

Beads

Ostrich feathers

Cedar wood

Cedar oil

Wine

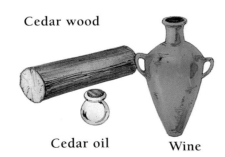

Horse

The King decided Egypt's foreign policy. He wrote directly to foreign rulers and there was a strict set of rules governing relations between kings. In the first half of the New Kingdom, the three strongest nations were the Egyptians, the Babylonians and the Mitanni (who were later replaced by the Hittites). These kings addressed one another as 'brother'. Lesser rulers addressed them as 'father'. They regularly exchanged letters and gifts through ambassadors. Egypt's main trade was with the eastern Mediterranean and Punt. Although ordinary merchants could operate independently, the bulk of Egypt's trade was carried out on the orders of the King. Egypt's gold, linen, papyrus, grain, wine, perfumes, furniture and jewellery were exchanged for silver, copper, timber, slaves, horses, ivory, resin, oils and incense.

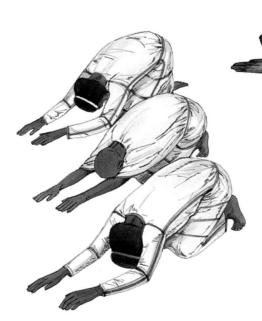

PRECIOUS INCENSE
No temple ceremony or funeral could be held without burning incense. Its sweet-smelling clouds of smoke were thought to carry prayers to heaven. It was also widely used in perfumes and medicines. Some of Egypt's incense may have come from South Arabia, but most came from the land of Punt.

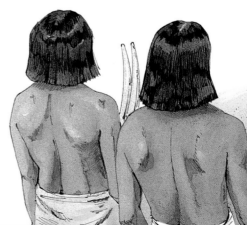

SNIFFING THE EARTH
When prisoners, rebels or even foreign ambassadors approached the King of Egypt, they were expected to touch the ground with their noses as a sign of humility and reverence. This was called 'sniffing the earth'.

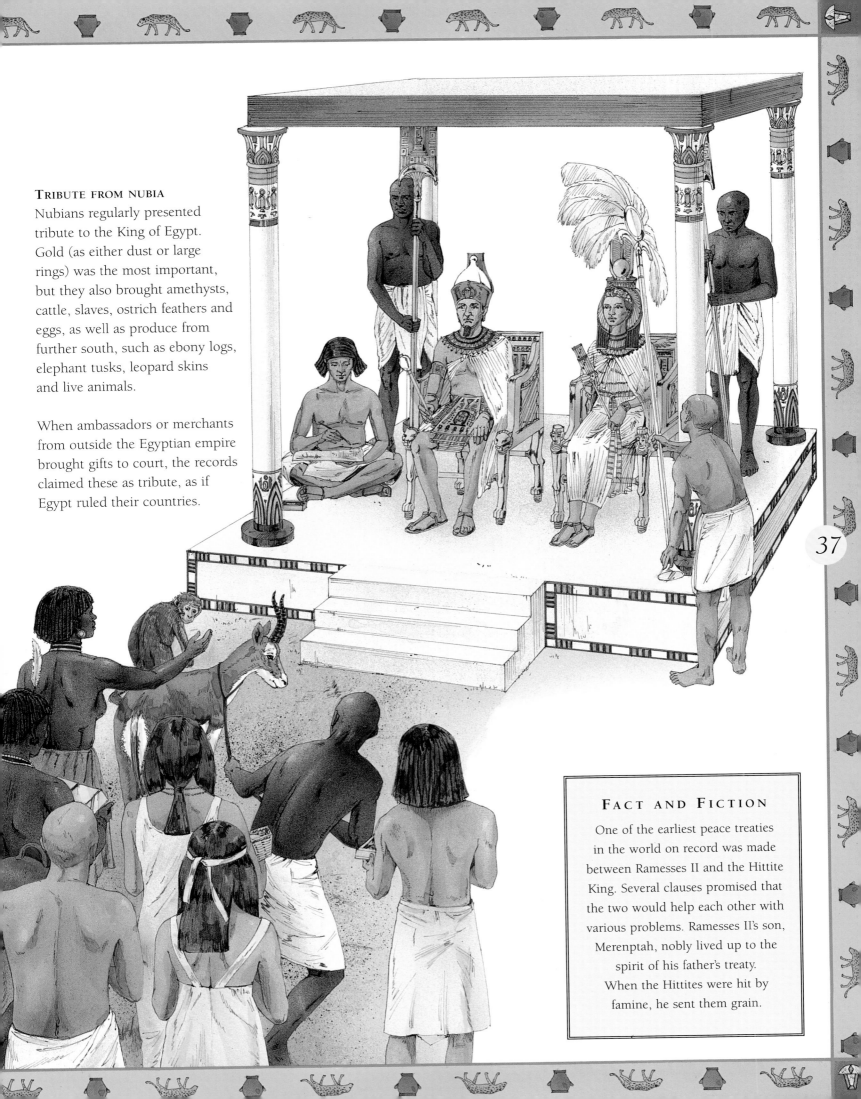

TRIBUTE FROM NUBIA

Nubians regularly presented tribute to the King of Egypt. Gold (as either dust or large rings) was the most important, but they also brought amethysts, cattle, slaves, ostrich feathers and eggs, as well as produce from further south, such as ebony logs, elephant tusks, leopard skins and live animals.

When ambassadors or merchants from outside the Egyptian empire brought gifts to court, the records claimed these as tribute, as if Egypt ruled their countries.

FACT AND FICTION

One of the earliest peace treaties in the world on record was made between Ramesses II and the Hittite King. Several clauses promised that the two would help each other with various problems. Ramesses II's son, Merenptah, nobly lived up to the spirit of his father's treaty. When the Hittites were hit by famine, he sent them grain.

T HE KING'S PEOPLE

The King towered unique and alone above everyone else in Egypt. Even his family was not in the same class. All his subjects served him by working for him – from the rich noblemen with important offices, down through the middle classes to the peasants, who were the majority of the population. Below them came the landless laborers and finally the slaves. The key to success in Egypt was being able to read and write. If a peasant family could pay for their son to go to school, then talent and hard work could lead to promotion, even to becoming Vizier.

EGYPTIAN WOMEN

Egyptian women were treated with great respect. Although they were not allowed to hold government office, they could hold jobs at court and be priestesses. There were also many skilled craftswomen. Women could own businesses, run farms and help their husbands with their work. They had full legal rights and control over their property. They could divorce their husbands and remarry if they wished.

CHILDREN

Children were seen as a great blessing. When they grew up, they were expected to care for their parents and provide offerings for them in the Next World. Childless couples prayed to gods, made offerings, saw doctors and consulted magicians. If everything else failed, they could adopt.

SLAVES

Slaves had certain rights and could own property. Favored household slaves could do well and gain their freedom. Some were even adopted by childless couples. Those working in mines and on building sites were treated more harshly.

TOMB ROBBERY

Tomb robbery was a sure sign of weak government. At the end of the Twentieth Dynasty, gangs of robbers were well organized with transport, hideaways and places to buy and sell their loot. They bribed officials to ignore their activities or to release them if arrested.

FACT AND FICTION

Egyptian tomb builders were not down-trodden slaves, as so often shown in films. However, in the Twentieth Dynasty, due to inefficient officials, the royal tomb workers were not paid their wages – which were in food and goods – for several weeks. They went on strike and held sit-ins and protests at temples.

39

THE KING JOINS THE GODS

In death, as in life, the King was unique. As a god, his spirit had to be launched into heaven to join his divine relatives. As a man, his body had to be preserved by mummification and provided with everything that would keep him in comfort for eternity. Only the Royal Family and the rich could afford the full mummification process, which took 70 days. The brain and internal organs were removed and the body was covered with natron salt for 40 days to dry it out. It was rubbed then with scented oil, packed with natron, linen, spices and resin. Gold covers were put over the fingers and toes and gold sandals on the feet. The body was wrapped in hundreds of metres of linen, with jewels and amulets placed among the layers.

Tutankhamun's shrine, which covered his canopic chest

THE KING'S BA
One part of the dead King's soul, called the ba, was pictured as a bird with the King's head. When released by priests' prayers and rituals, it could swoop to earth to enjoy the daily offerings made to him, or soar to the 'Imperishable Stars' – the North Pole Star and those that never sink below the horizon.

CANOPIC CHEST
The internal organs were also dried out in natron, wrapped and stored in pots called canopic jars. These were placed in a decorated canopic chest, which, in turn, might be placed in a magnificent shrine.

Tutankhamun's canopic chest and jars

FACT AND FICTION

In the Middle Ages, Europeans thought that ground-up mummies made excellent medicine! King Francis I of France had some as a daily tonic. Egyptian merchants organised the mummy robberies. It is said that, when supplies ran low, they killed slaves and turned them into mummies to meet the demand.

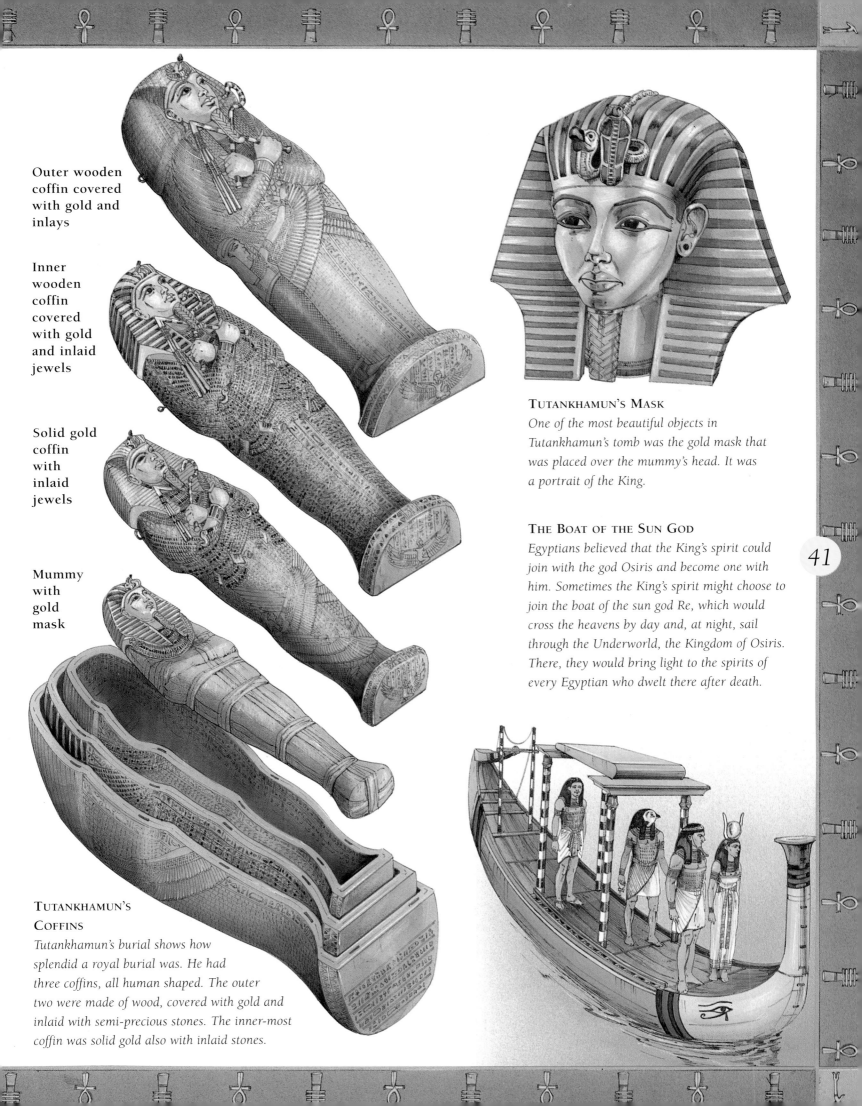

Outer wooden coffin covered with gold and inlays

Inner wooden coffin covered with gold and inlaid jewels

Solid gold coffin with inlaid jewels

Mummy with gold mask

TUTANKHAMUN'S MASK

One of the most beautiful objects in Tutankhamun's tomb was the gold mask that was placed over the mummy's head. It was a portrait of the King.

THE BOAT OF THE SUN GOD

Egyptians believed that the King's spirit could join with the god Osiris and become one with him. Sometimes the King's spirit might choose to join the boat of the sun god Re, which would cross the heavens by day and, at night, sail through the Underworld, the Kingdom of Osiris. There, they would bring light to the spirits of every Egyptian who dwelt there after death.

TUTANKHAMUN'S COFFINS

Tutankhamun's burial shows how splendid a royal burial was. He had three coffins, all human shaped. The outer two were made of wood, covered with gold and inlaid with semi-precious stones. The inner-most coffin was solid gold also with inlaid stones.

SAND TO PYRAMIDS

The earliest Egyptian graves were scoops in the sand with stones piled on top. Ordinary Egyptians were always buried like this, wrapped in linen or leather, or put in wooden or reed coffins. They were buried with food and sometimes with tools. Chieftains and, later, kings felt they needed grand tombs to display their power. These tombs needed to be big enough to hold all the goods that kings thought they would use in the Next World.

MASTABAS

Mastabas were the earliest large tombs. They were large rectangular buildings made of mud bricks, with chambers both inside and underneath. These were used from the end of the Predynastic Period to the end of the Second Dynasty. The one below was built at Abydos.

Mastaba

The true pyramid contained a burial chamber. From the late Fifth Dynasty there were magic spells carved on the tomb's walls to help the king in the Next World.

Queen's pyramid

Mortuary temple

Causeway

Mastabas for noblemen

STEP PYRAMID

In the Third Dynasty, King Zoser's chief minister, Imhotep, decided to build the King a monument in stone. It started as a single mastaba, then he built others on top and so invented the world's first pyramid, the Step Pyramid at Sakkara. This was thought to represent a ladder by which the Kings could climb to the northern 'Imperishable Stars'.

TRUE PYRAMID

From the Fourth Dynasty onwards, pyramids were built with straight sides. These are thought to represent sunbeams forming ramps, up which the King could walk to join the sun god Re in his boat. These 'true pyramids' were used for royal burials until the beginning of the New Kingdom.

ANUBIS

The chief embalmer wore the mask of Anubis, god of embalming, and said prayers and spells over the mummy.

LECTOR PRIEST

Throughout the mummification, lector priests chanted rituals that would help the King on his journey to the Next World.

'TWO KITES'

Wailing royal ladies knelt at the ends of the coffin. They represented Nephthys and Isis mourning their brother, the god Osiris.

SEM PRIEST

Just before burial, the new King, as sem (funeral) priest, conducted a ceremony, to give the dead King power of speech and movement.

KA PRIEST

The ka (soul) priest made daily offerings of food, drink, incense and flowers for the King's spirit at the mortuary temple.

FACT AND FICTION

King Khufu's pyramid was under construction throughout his reign of 24 years. Its sides align almost perfectly to the points of the compass. It contains over 2,300,000 blocks. The average block weighs 2.5 tons and the biggest ones weigh up to 15 tons. In the flood season, between 20,000 and 100,000 men helped haul the blocks into place.

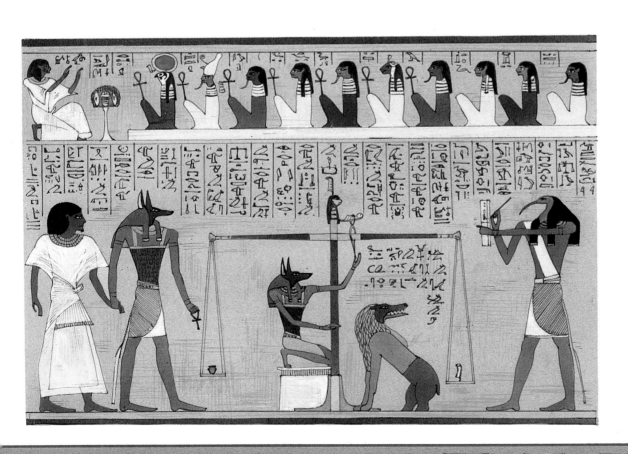

WEIGHING THE HEART

The King's passage to join the gods was assured, but his subjects had to face the Judgment Hall of Osiris. Here, before Osiris, a person's heart was weighed against the feather of truth.

A sinful heart unbalanced the scales and the guilty spirit was gobbled up by a monster. The heart of a good person was as light as the feather, and its good spirit could enter the wonderful Kingdom of Osiris, which was considered to be identical to Egypt, but perfect.

THE VALLEY OF THE KINGS

TUTANKHAMUN'S TOMB

After Tutankhamun's funeral, workmen waited until the royal mourners had left to block the doors and the entrance. The last person out of each room was a priest. He walked backwards, brushing away any traces of footprints, so that demons could not use them to invade the tomb. Tutankhamun's riches are renowned, even though he reigned for only ten years, died before he was 20 and was buried in a small tomb. Think of what riches must have been inside the tombs of longer-reigning and more successful Pharaohs!

In the troubles during the First and Second Intermediate Periods, all the pyramids were robbed, so New Kingdom Kings gave up building them. Instead, they had tombs cut into the cliffs of a valley on the west bank of the Nile, opposite their capital, Thebes. This area became known as the Valley of the Kings. Skilled, very well-paid workmen cut and decorated these royal tombs. A village was built for them – now called Deir el Medinah. Egypt was rich from its trade and tribute from its empire, so the royal tombs were filled with breathtaking treasures. At the end of the New Kingdom, law and order broke down and the tombs were not guarded properly. Most of them were robbed and several mummies destroyed. Priests secretly reburied those that survived in two tombs. These were not disturbed until the end of the nineteenth century.

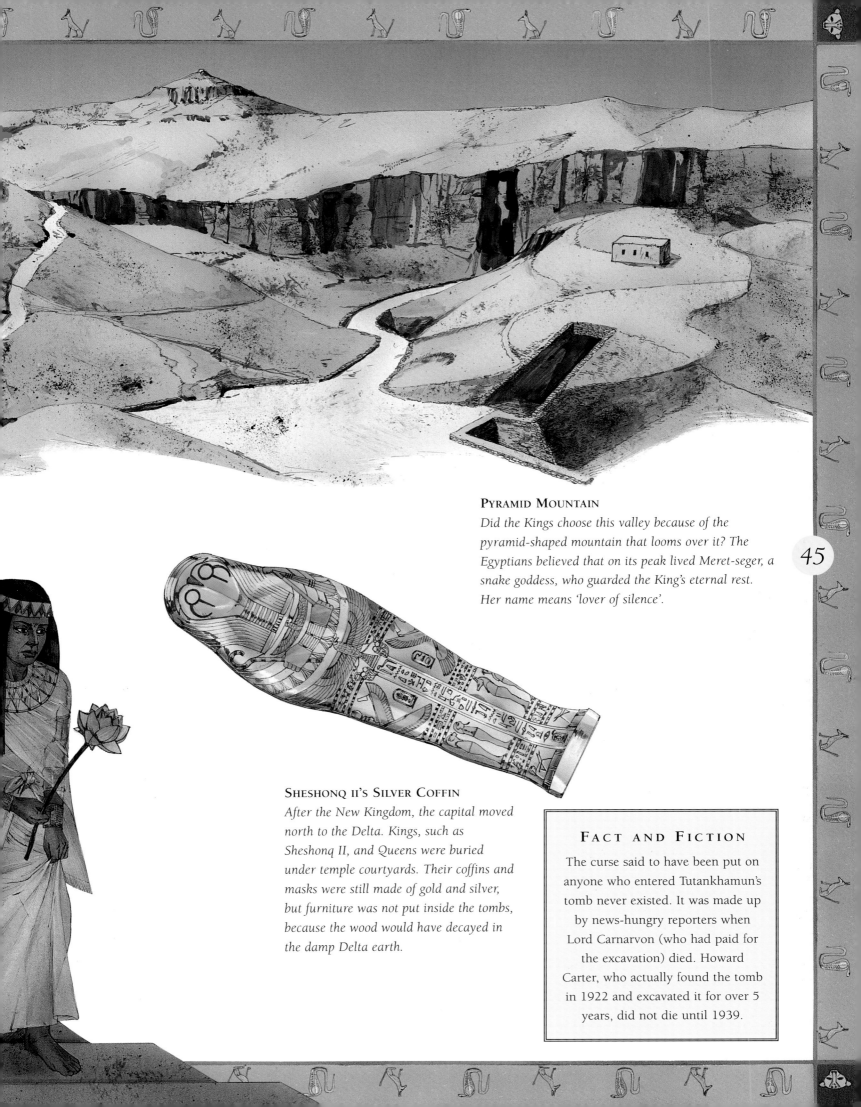

PYRAMID MOUNTAIN

Did the Kings choose this valley because of the pyramid-shaped mountain that looms over it? The Egyptians believed that on its peak lived Meret-seger, a snake goddess, who guarded the King's eternal rest. Her name means 'lover of silence'.

SHESHONQ II'S SILVER COFFIN

After the New Kingdom, the capital moved north to the Delta. Kings, such as Sheshonq II, and Queens were buried under temple courtyards. Their coffins and masks were still made of gold and silver, but furniture was not put inside the tombs, because the wood would have decayed in the damp Delta earth.

FACT AND FICTION

The curse said to have been put on anyone who entered Tutankhamun's tomb never existed. It was made up by news-hungry reporters when Lord Carnarvon (who had paid for the excavation) died. Howard Carter, who actually found the tomb in 1922 and excavated it for over 5 years, did not die until 1939.

WHO'S WHO

Scorpion (PREDYNASTIC)
The King of Upper Egypt. He dedicated offerings to the temple at Hierakonpolis.

Narmer (FIRST DYNASTY)
Egyptian Kings had two names, so Narmer may also be Menes, the King who united Egypt and built Memphis as its capital.

Imhotep (THIRD DYNASTY)
A top official, High Priest and the architect who designed the first step pyramid for King Zoser at Sakkara. He is also said to have been a doctor and to have reformed the calendar and the writing system. He was later worshipped as a god.

Khufu (FOURTH DYNASTY)
Builder of the Great Pyramid at Gizah. His is the first royal name found at the trading post at Buhen in Nubia.

Khafre (FOURTH DYNASTY)
Khafre was successful in his struggle for his father Khufu's throne. He built the second pyramid at Gizah and the Sphinx.

Pepi II (SIXTH DYNASTY)
Pepi had the longest recorded reign in history. He came to the throne aged 6, and reigned for 94 years! As he grew older, his control weakened. Many of his sons died before him, so the succession was disputed. As a result, the Old Kingdom collapsed.

Mentuhotep II (2055 - 2004 BC)
His family were Nomarchs (district governors) of Thebes and rivals of the Tenth Dynasty. Mentuhotep defeated them, re-united Egypt and worked to restore its greatness.

Amenemhat I (1985 - 1955 BC)
Top official in the Eleventh Dynasty, he became King after a civil war. His successful reign ended when he was killed in a conspiracy. He was succeeded by Senusret I, his chosen heir, whom he had already crowned during his lifetime.

Senusret III (1874 - 1855 BC)
A great warrior, who reached the 3rd Cataract, fought the Kushites and strengthened the frontier fortresses. At home, he re-organised the government and reduced the power of the Nomarchs.

Seqenenre Tao II (C.1560 BC)
King in Thebes and leader of the opposition to the Hyksos. His mummy shows that he died a violent death, either fighting the Hyksos or from assassination.

Ahmose (1550 - 1526 BC)
The King who finally drove out the Hyksos and started the conquest of the empire. He came to the throne as a child, with his mother, Ah-hotep, as Regent.

Hatshepsut (1478 - 1458 BC)
Heiress to the royal line, she married her half-brother, Tuthmosis II. When he died, his son by a minor wife became Tuthmosis III. However, Hapshepsut made herself his

co-'King' and ruled for 20 years. She seems to have led her soldiers into battle in Nubia and restarted up trade with Punt. She had a spectacular funeral temple built for her at Deir el-Bahari.

Tuthmosis III
(1479 - 1425 BC)
Came to the throne as a boy of about 10, Tuthmosis was kept

in the background by Hatshepsut for the 20 years of her reign. He eventually became the greatest of Egypt's warrior Kings, with more than 17 successful campaigns in Nubia and Canaan. He married Hatshepsut's daughter.

Amenhotep II (1425 - 1401 BC)
Warrior and sportsman. He left several records, telling of his victories, his feats as a hunter and a rower, his horsemanship and his strength.

Tiy
Wife and probably cousin of Amenhotep III. The favourite of her husband's many wives, she played an important role in government. Her second son was the 'heretic' Pharaoh, Akhenaten.

Akhenaten (1352 - 1338 BC)
Believing there to be only one god, Aten, Amenhotep IV renamed himself Akhenaten, to honour his god. He banned the worship of other gods and built a new capital at Amarna. He concentrated on religious matters at the expense of the empire. Much of the northern part was captured by the Hittites. After his death, his buildings were torn down, the old gods brought back and Amarna abandoned. It was forbidden to even mention his name.

Nefertiti

Wife and possible cousin of Akhenaten. They had six daughters, but no sons. Nefertiti seems to have become 'King' towards the end of his reign. Her fate after his death is unknown.

Tutankhamun

(1336 - 1327 BC)
Son of Akhenaten and a minor wife. He came to the throne at about age 10 and died at the early age of 20. He became famous when his tomb was found, intact, by Howard Carter in 1922.

Ramesses II

(1279 -1212 BC)
He fought the Hittites and claimed great victories. However, neither side could win, so they made peace. Ramesses launched a massive building program, including the building of rock-cut temple at Abu Simbel, in Nubia. He also often put his names on existing buildings, as if he had built them. He had many wives and hundreds of children. He reigned 67 years and there was dispute among his successors.

Merenptah (1212 - 1202 BC)

Thirteenth son of Ramesses II, Merenptah became King, because his twelve elder brothers had died before him during their father's long reign. When the Hittites were suffering from a famine, he sent them food – the first example of international famine relief.

Tawosret (1196 - 1188 BC)

Daughter of Merenptah and wife of her brother, Seti II. When Seti died young, Tawosret was married to a rival prince. When he died as well, she became 'King'.

Ramesses III (1184 - 1154 BC)

He saved Egypt from the Sea Peoples, who had wiped out the Hittites and disrupted trade contacts. Egypt suffered from the loss of trade, prices rose and the first recorded strikes occurred. There was a plot to put a minor wife's son on the throne. The attempt failed, and Ramesses died soon after.

Ramesses XI (1098 - 1069 BC)

Last King of his dynasty. His reign was troubled by tomb robberies, inefficient government and a war between the high priest of Amun and the Viceroy of Kush. Kush became independent and Ramesses' daughter married the man who became the first King of the Twenty-first Dynasty.

Sheshonq I (945 - 924 BC)

Descended from Libyan mercenaries, his family married into the Egyptian nobility. His son married the heiress of the Twenty-first Dynasty and Sheshonq seized the throne. He invaded Judah and took the treasures of the Temple of Jerusalem.

Piankhy I (TWENTY-FIFTH DYNASTY)

Nubian King who conquered Egypt. He claimed he came to restore the pure worship of Amun. He was outraged after besieging a town to find that his enemy had let his horses suffer.

Psamtek I (664 - 610 BC)

Nobleman who co-operated with the Assyrians to drive out the Nubian Kings, then abandoned the Assyrians and made himself King. He ruled from Saïs and set about restoring Egypt's prosperity and prestige.

Nectanebo II (380 - 362 BC)

Ruler after the Persians had left, he kept Egypt at peace, restored its wealth and started building several temples. He was said to have been a great magician.

Ptolemy I (305 - 282 BC)

One of Alexander's generals, Ptolemy held Egypt after Alexander's death and founded a dynasty. He and his successors promoted Egypt's trade and prosperity and built many temples.

Cleopatra VII (51 - 30 BC)

The last Pharaoh. She was an able ruler who wanted to restore Egypt's empire. To do so, she needed Rome's alliance and was supported by two great generals, Julius Caesar and Mark Antony. During the civil war, Octavius (later Emperor Augustus) declared war on Antony and Cleopatra. When finally defeated, they both chose to commit suicide rather than surrender.

INDEX

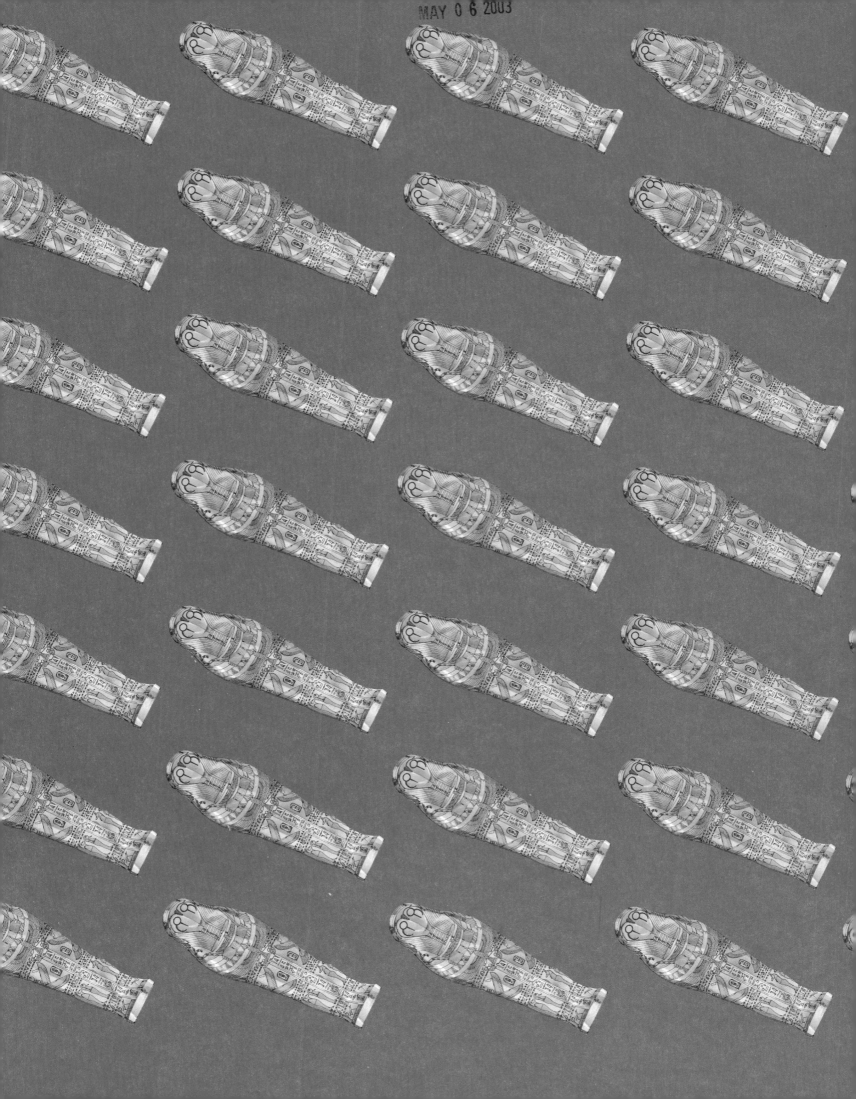